MATH IN OUR WORLD

USING

DIVISION

AT SPORTS CAMP

By Linda Bussell

Reading consultant: Susan Nations, M.Ed.,
author/literacy coach/consultant in literacy development
Math consultant: Rhea Stewart, M.A., mathematics content specialist

WEEKLY READER®
PUBLISHING

Please visit our web site at **www.garethstevens.com**
For a free color catalog describing our list of high-quality books,
call 1-800-542-2595 (USA) or 1-800-387-3178 (Canada). Our fax: 1-877-542-2596

Library of Congress Cataloging-in-Publication Data
Bussell, Linda.
      Using division at sports camp / by Linda Bussell.
         p. cm. — (Math in our world level 3)
      Includes bibliographical references and index.
      ISBN-10: 0-8368-9288-7 — ISBN-13: 978-0-8368-9288-8 (lib. bdg.)
      ISBN-10: 0-8368-9387-5 — ISBN-13: 978-0-8368-9387-8 (softcover)
      1. Division—Juvenile literature. 2. Sports camps—Juvenile literature. I. Title.
QA115.B975   2009
513.2'14—dc22   2008012129

This edition first published in 2009 by
Weekly Reader® Books
An Imprint of Gareth Stevens Publishing
1 Reader's Digest Road
Pleasantville, NY 10570-7000 USA

Creative Director: Lisa Donovan
Designer: Amelia Favazza, *Studio Montage*
Copy Editor: Susan Labella
Photo Researcher: Kim Babbitt

Photo Credits: cover, title page, pp. 18, 20, 21: Bob Daemmrich/Photo Edit;
pp. 4, 11: Artville; p. 5, 12: David Young-Wolff/Photo Edit; pp. 6, 16: BananaStock;
pp. 8, 17: Photodisc; p. 10: Frank Siteman/Photo Edit; p. 14: Hemera Technologies

Printed in the United States

1 2 3 4 5 6 7 8 9 10 09 08

Table of Contents

Words that appear in the glossary are printed in **boldface** type the first time they occur in the text.

Chapter 1

Eagles, Falcons, and Hawks

It is summer. Sports camp starts today, and the campers are excited. They have many choices. They will play tennis, volleyball, and soccer. They will run, hike, and swim.

There are 336 campers in all. They must **divide** into smaller groups to play sports.

Bobby is one of 3 leaders at the camp. He divides the campers into 3 equal groups. Each group will have its own leader. Bobby divides 336 by 3. He writes this on the board:

$$\frac{112}{3\overline{\smash{)}336}}$$

There are 112 campers in each group, and each group will have its own name.

The 3 groups are named the Eagles, the Falcons, and the Hawks. They will take turns playing sports. Then there will be enough equipment for everyone.

To start, the Eagles will play volleyball. The Falcons will play tennis. The Hawks will play soccer. Some campers will hike, swim, and run, too.

The leaders make 3 lists. They add the name of each camper to a list. That means they add 112 names to each list. When they are done, each of the 336 campers will be in a group.

The teams take turns playing sports. The Falcons play tennis first!

5

Chapter 2

Choosing Teams

Next, the leaders organize the groups. Some of the campers help them. They divide everyone into teams.

James and Rebecca help the Falcons. They make teams for doubles tennis. There are 2 players on each team. They need to find out how many teams to make, so they divide 112 by 2.

The Falcons will have 56 teams for doubles tennis. James lists the numbers from 1 to 56. Rebecca reads the names of the campers, and James writes 2 names next to each number. Soon, they have a list of 56 teams.

James and Rebecca figure out
how many doubles tennis teams
they need to make.

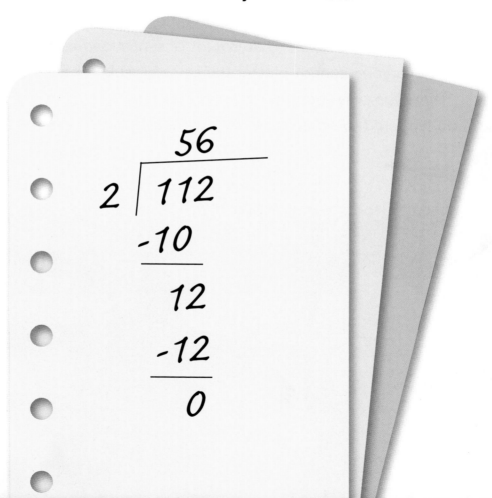

$$
\begin{array}{r}
56 \\
2\overline{)112} \\
-10 \\
\hline
12 \\
-12 \\
\hline
0
\end{array}
$$

James and Rebecca make a schedule for the doubles tennis games. Two teams will play each game.

James divides 56 by 2.

"If everyone plays at the same time, there will be 28 games!" James says. "That is a lot of tennis games."

"Everyone cannot play at the same time," Rebecca says. "There are only 7 tennis courts. How many groups of games do we need to schedule so everyone can play?" she asks.

The Falcons need to play
28 games of tennis so everyone
on the team has a turn.

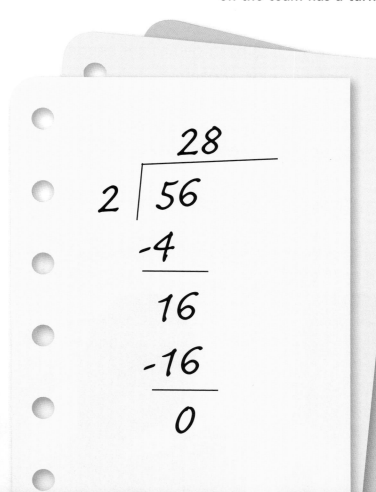

$$2\overline{)56}$$

28

−4

16

−16

0

"I know what to do," says James. He writes this on the white board:

28 ÷ 7 = 4

"We have 28 games of tennis to play. We have 7 courts. To find out how many groups of games are needed, I divided 28 by 7. We need 4 groups of games."

They put teams of 2 into game groups.

"This schedule looks great," Bobby says. "I will use this to make schedules for the other activities. Do you want to help me?"

"Yes!" say James and Rebecca.

The camp has 7 tennis courts, so the Falcons need to play 4 rounds of tennis to play 28 games in all.

Chapter 3

Everybody Gets to Play!

William and Braden are in the Eagles group. The 2 campers help their leader, Katie, make a game schedule. They divide the Eagles into teams for volleyball. There are 6 players on a volleyball team. There are 112 Eagles. William says they should divide 112 by 6. The **quotient** will tell them how many teams to make. Braden writes:

112 ÷ 6 = 18 r4

"We need to make 18 teams," says Braden.

"There is a **remainder** of 4," says William. "That is not enough players to make another team of 6."

They add an extra player to 4 teams. The players will take turns.

The Hawks plan their soccer teams. Brianna and Isabella are on the Hawks. They help their leader, Taylor. They divide the Hawks into teams for soccer.

There are 112 Hawks. Each team is allowed to put 7 players on the field at one time.

"How many teams will we have if there are 7 players on a team?" asks Isabella.

She divides 112 by 7.

112 ÷ 7 = 16

"The quotient is 16. There will be 16 teams of 7 players each," she says.

**The Hawks play soccer first.
They plan how to divide into teams.**

Isabella divides 112 campers into soccer teams.

$$\begin{array}{r} 16 \\ 7\overline{)112} \\ -7 \\ \hline 42 \\ 42 \\ \hline 0 \end{array}$$

We should have more than 7 players on each team," says Brianna. "Then players can take a break when they get tired."

"That is fine," says Taylor. "However, the rules say there can be no more than 10 players on a team."

Isabella says, "If we place 10 players on each team, we will have 11 teams. There will be 2 players left." She shows her work.

"That won't work," says Brianna. "We need to try something else."

Brianna and Isabella think more about how they can divide the teams.

If the Hawks form 11 teams from the group of 112 campers, then 2 teams will have 11 players. That is against the rules.

Isabella and Brianna decide to create 12 teams.

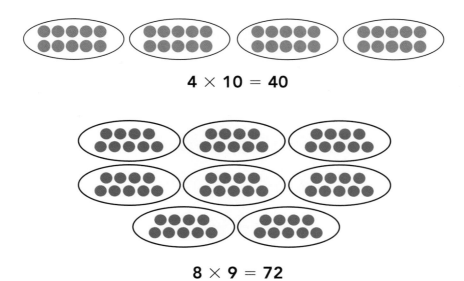

4 × 10 = 40

8 × 9 = 72

Four teams will have 10 players each, and 8 teams will have 9 players each.

40 + 72 = 112

Everyone gets to play!

The campers have a busy week. They play tennis, volleyball, and soccer. They hike, run and swim. They have lots of fun.

Chapter 4

Sports Festival

On the last day of camp, the campers have a sports festival. It is time to get ready. The campers organize the events.

They sign up for the sports they want to play. There is soccer, volleyball, and tennis. Some campers sign up for swimming. Others sign up for running.

The most popular event is the 100-meter race. A total of 123 campers sign up to run.

There are too many runners to run at one time. The track only has 8 lanes. Eight runners can run at a time.

"We can divide the runners into smaller groups," Braden says. "These smaller groups are called **heats**. Each heat is a race. The winner of each heat will race against the winners of other heats."

Braden and Isabella divide runners into heats of 8. Braden writes:

123 ÷ 8 = 15 r3

"We will need at least 16 heats," he says. "We can have 15 heats with 8 runners each. We can have 1 heat with only 3 runners."

More than 120 campers want to race! Braden and Isabella divide runners into heats.

"It will be more fun if there are more runners in the last heat," says Isabella. "I have an idea."

"We can take 1 runner from each of 4 heats. We can add these 4 runners to the heat that has only 3 runners," she says.

Isabella writes on the board:

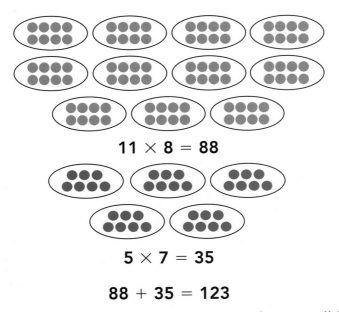

$11 \times 8 = 88$

$5 \times 7 = 35$

$88 + 35 = 123$

"Eleven heats will have 8 runners. Five heats will have 7 runners. Everyone who wants to run will get to race," says Isabella.

This is just the start of the 100-meter race, though.

After 16 heats, the winner from each heat will race again. These races will be the **semifinals**.

"There will be 16 runners in the semifinals. There will be 8 runners in each semifinal heat," said Braden. He writes:

16 ÷ 8 = 2

"There will be 2 semifinal heats," he says. "The winners of the 2 semifinal heats will run in the final race. The winner of the final race will be the winner of the 100-meter race."

Winners of the heats will race against each other in semifinal races.

The plans for the sports festival are complete. The campers have many events planned. They have also planned hikes and water games for their guests.

The campers' families and friends come to the sports festival. Everyone has fun. Campers play the championship games for soccer and volleyball in the afternoon.

The 100-meter race is the final event of the day. The finish is very close, almost a tie. The tired runners shake hands. Their friends cheer. The festival ends a great week of fun and fitness.

The 100-meter race is the last event of the day. The runners almost tie!

21

What Did You Learn?

(1) The new soccer league had 72 players sign up. The league wants 9 players to a team. How many teams will there be?

(2) For Field Day, 67 third graders want to run in the long-distance race. Only 7 runners can race at a time. How many races are needed for everyone to run?

Glossary

divide: to separate items into equal groups. Division is the opposite operation of multiplication.

heat: one of a series of races in sports

quotient: the number, not including the remainder, that results from division.
In **48 ÷ 8 = 6, 6** is the quotient.

remainder: the amount left over when a number cannot be divided evenly

semifinals: the heats that are run to decide who will be in the final race. The winners of the semifinal heats will be in the final race.

Index

About the Author

Linda Bussell has written and designed books, supplemental learning materials, educational games, and software programs for children and young adults. She lives with her family in San Diego, California.